DRUGS **the facts about**

MARIJUANA

DRUGS the facts about

MARIJUANA

TED GOTTFRIED

BENCHMARK BOOKS

MARSHALL CAVENDISH
NEW YORK

For Harriet

Series Consultant: Dr. Amy Kohn, Chief Executive Officer, YWCA of White Plains and Central Westchester, New York. Thanks to John M. Roll, PhD, Director of Behavioral Pharmacology at UCLA Integrated Substance Abuse Programs, for his expert reading of this manuscript.

Acknowledgments

I am grateful to personnel of the Humanities and Social Sciences Library and the Mid-Manhattan Library of the New York Public Library, the Queens Borough Public Library, the Drug Enforcement Administration, the National Institute on Drug Abuse, the National Organization for the Reform of Marijuana Laws, the Office of National Drug Control Policy Clearinghouse, the Partnership for a Drug-Free America, and many others for aid in gathering material for this book. Also, gratitude and much love to my wife, Harriet Gottfried, who—as always—read and critiqued the manuscript. Her help was invaluable, but any shortcomings in the work are mine alone
T. G.

Benchmark Books
Marshall Cavendish
99 White Plains Road
Tarrytown, NY 10591-9001
www.marshallcavendish.us

Text copyright © 2005 by Marshall Cavendish Corporation
Illustrations copyright © 2005 by Marshall Cavendish Corporation

Library of Congress Cataloging-in-Publication Data

Gottfried, Ted.
The facts about marijuana / by Ted Gottfried.
p. cm. — (Drugs)
Includes bibliographical references and index.
ISBN 0-7614-1806-7
1. Marijuana—Juvenile literature. 2. Marijuana abuse—Juvenile literature. 3. Marijuana—Law and legislation—United States—Juvenile literature. I. Title. II. Series: Drugs (Benchmark Books (Firm))

HV5822.M3G68 2005
362.29'5—dc22
2004005578

Photo research by Joan Meisel
Cover photo: Boucharlat/Photo Researchers, Inc.
Corbis: Bettmann, 13, 16, 22; Reuters, 49; Roy Morsch, 74. Getty Images: Don Farrall, 6;
Sean Gallup, 24; Paul S. Howell, 40; Tim Boyle, 44; Justin Sullivan, 56, 71; Spencer Platt, 58;
Jerry Laizure, 77. Photo Researchers, Inc.: Boucharlat, 1, 3

CONTENTS

THE MARIJUANA PLANT, ALSO KNOWN AS THE INDIAN HEMP PLANT (CANNABIS SATIVA), GROWS WILD IN DRY, HILLY REGIONS WITH MODERATE CLIMATES IN MANY PARTS OF THE WORLD. IT SOMETIMES REACHES HEIGHTS OF 16 FEET (4.8 METERS). ALTHOUGH USED AS A "PLEASURE DRUG" SINCE 3000 B.C.E., MARIJUANA MAY DISORIENT USERS AND HAVE UNPLEASANT SIDE EFFECTS.

1 What Is Marijuana?

LOTS OF THINGS are said about marijuana. Some are negative, some positive, most more opinion than fact. There is one thing, however, that all can agree on: in the United States of America today, marijuana is illegal.

You can go to jail for using it. You can go to jail for selling it. You can go to jail for having it in your possession. A combination of federal and state laws say so. As we discuss the pros and cons of the issues surrounding marijuana, you should never lose track of this. The rights and wrongs of legalizing marijuana, of permitting its medical use, of criminalizing those who use it, of calling it a gateway drug, and of many other issues covered in this book may be argued in our free society. But the bottom line is that selling, possessing, and using pot is a crime, and if you do the crime, then you may do the time in prison.

The Indian Hemp Plant

That was not always the case, even in the United States. In the five thousand years of recorded marijuana use, it has only been illegal in the U.S. since 1937. The earliest known use of marijuana took place in China and Central Asia in 3000 B.C.E. It quickly came into popular use in India and the Near East. In India it acquired its name—the Indian hemp plant *(Cannabis sativa)*—and its reputation as a pleasure drug.

The Indian hemp plant grows to a height of up to 16 feet (4.8 meters). The varieties used to produce marijuana, however, are much shorter and have multiple branches. The resin exuded by the hemp plant contains the substance tetrahydrocannabinol, or THC, which is responsible for the effects marijuana has on users. THC is found to varying degrees in all the parts of the plant, including the flowering tops, the fruit pods, the seeds, the leaves, the stems, and the bark. The plants grow in temperate climates and do best in dry, hilly lands.

Hashish is the most potent form of marijuana. Mostly grown in North Africa, it is eight times as strong as the average marijuana used in the United States. Rich in THC distilled from the resin of the hemp plant, hashish looks like a congealed brown lump of powder. The darker brown the lump is, the more potent the hashish.

Drug of the Assassins

Legend has it that hashish was named after Hasan-ibn-Sabah, the head of a murderous sect called *fidais,* "the devoted ones." Hasan had carved a fortress out of a mountain in Persia, and was feared locally as the "Old Man of the Mountains." Combining religion with outlawry, Hasan's fidais preyed on the rich caravans that traveled the area, as well as on the local inhabitants.

Their activities were chronicled by the famous explorer Marco Polo. According to Polo's and other accounts, Hasan's stronghold was a training camp for assassins who were promised entry to paradise in exchange for serving him. Recruits were escorted to a garden where they were given hashish and entertained by sensual and obliging dancing girls. Afterward they were brought to Hasan, who promised them more visits to the garden if they carried out his orders.

The fidais were not allowed to take hashish before going out on a mission. Hasan evidently recognized that hashish would affect the judgment and reflexes needed to carry out their murderous assignments. One by one, they infiltrated themselves into a caravan's camp to wait for the order to strike. Despite the fact that they did not use hashish while on an assignment, they were called the hashishers, known for the wild frenzies and merciless brutality of their attacks.

A Major Crop

Hashish and Persian assassins aside, there is little in the history of marijuana to indicate the violence with which it would become identified in the latter half of twentieth-century America. Depending on the source, there are different accounts of just how it emerged in North America. According to one version, marijuana grows wild on our continent, and was used by American Indians long before the arrival of European colonists for religious ceremonies, as medicine, and as a prebattle smoke to calm the nerves. Others believe that marijuana was brought into Spain from Morocco by sailors on merchant ships. In 1545 the Spanish brought it to the New World. Still another account has the English importing marijuana from Russia, Asia, and North Africa, introducing it to the Jamestown Colony in North America in 1611.

Whatever the truth—or combination of truths— by 1629 hemp plants from which marijuana could be derived had become a major crop for American colonists. It was their main source of raw material for paper, clothing, and rope. By 1762 hemp production was so necessary a part of the American colonies' economy that the Virginia legislature passed a law imposing penalties on farms that did not grow hemp. George Washington was an early hemp farmer and kept records about the quality and productiveness of his hemp fields. There is, however, no truth to the later rumors that he did this in order to increase the potency of the THC in the resin of the plants. Nor is there any evidence that Washington ever smoked pot.

In 1793, with the invention of the cotton gin,

hemp farmers like Washington began to cut back on their hemp production. The cotton gin made the separation of cotton fiber from the plant much easier. As a result, it became cheaper and easier to make clothes from cotton than from hemp. Farmers found it more profitable to grow cotton. Following the Civil War, many of the remaining hemp plantations switched to growing tobacco.

Medical History

In 1854 the *United States Pharmacopeia*—the official book of drugs and medicines, their uses and medicinal values—included marijuana in its listings. As the use of hemp for fiber decreased, the medicinal use of marijuana from hemp plants increased. While it never became as widely (and legally) used as laudanum, which contained opium, cannabis—as marijuana was known medicinally—was used during the last half of the nineteenth century to treat gout, migraine headaches, rheumatism, hysteria, depression, loss of appetite, childbirth pains, and many other conditions.

The use of marijuana as medicine began to decline in the early 1900s. A major reason for this was the difficulty of regulating the dosage. There are many different varieties of the cannabis plant, and they produce different strengths of THC, which often result in widely varying levels and periods of effectiveness. There was also the factor of differing constitutions and general states of health among patients rendering the effects of marijuana treatment unpredictable. It should be noted that marijuana as a medicine was swallowed rather than smoked and that the THC in syrup form is far more powerful than that in the hemp fiber smoked in reefers.

Before World War I, the use of marijuana as a recreational drug wasn't common in the United States. Two things changed that. American soldiers came in contact with the drug in Europe, where it both reduced the stress in the trenches and heightened the pleasure of those short periods when they were granted leave. After the war the soldiers returned to a land where national Prohibition deprived them of liquor. Marijuana was a legal alternative to booze, and fast becoming a part of the liberated spirit of the Roaring Twenties.

Tea Pads and Pot Patrol

In the 1920s flappers (liberated dancing women in fringed skirts) showed their knees, college boys in beaver coats carried hip flasks filled with illegal whiskey, gangsters rubbed elbows with society debutantes, and the music was fast and stimulating. The music was jazz, and it defined the age. For Jazz Age musicians marijuana was literally a part of their music. So-called reefer songs became all the rage. The clouds of marijuana smoke that hung over late-hour jam sessions spread from the musicians to the customers and soon mingled with the cigarette smoke in the speakeasies, where illegal liquor was served.

WHILE CHARLESTON DANCERS WITH BARE KNEES KICKED OFF THE JAZZ AGE OF THE 1920S, REEFERS (HAND-ROLLED MARIJUANA CIGARETTES) MADE THEIR FIRST APPEARANCE CONTRIBUTING TO THE CLOUDS OF SMOKE FILLING SPEAKEASIES. THE LIQUOR SERVED DURING PROHIBITION WAS ILLEGAL, BUT THE POT WAS NOT.

Although marijuana was legal during this period, most of it was no longer being grown in the United States. Rather, it was imported from Cuba and Mexico. With the rise of jazz, marijuana began appearing in the clubs of New Orleans and Memphis and other southern port cities. Sometimes it was brought to the United States by Mexican migrant workers. Its popularity spread quickly to Chicago, New York, San Francisco, and lesser metropolises. So-called tea pads, similar to the opium dens found in the Chinese sections of New York and San Francisco, came into fashion. Here marijuana smokers could smoke and relax privately. By 1930 there were five hundred tea pads in New York City alone.

When Prohibition was repealed in 1933, attention turned to the increase in the use of marijuana. Public outrage was fueled by sensational newspaper accounts involving crime, sex, and reefer smoking. States began passing laws restricting shipping, selling, and in many cases using marijuana. By 1937 forty-six of the forty-eight states and the District of Columbia had passed antipot laws. That same year the federal Marihuana [sic] Tax Act was signed into law. It required persons dealing in marijuana to register with the government and pay a special tax. By regulating imports and sales, it also restricted the ability of Americans to purchase marijuana.

During the 1930s the Federal Bureau of Narcotics mounted a publicity campaign portraying marijuana as a menace. Despite this campaign, the number of tea pads increased. Many of them moved into former speakeasies. Government attention turned to the Mexican border, the point of entry for much of the marijuana in the U.S. By the end of World War II, seizures of marijuana had become the top priority for the U.S. border patrols. In 1945 more marijuana was seized at the Mexican border than was confiscated in the entire United States. Despite the seizures and although most Americans may have still associated marijuana with crazed, reefer-smoking jazz drummers, a considerable pot-smoking subculture had developed, and it was growing.

Smokin' Through the Sixties

The marijuana subculture grew throughout the 1950s and emerged with an in-your-face vengeance in the 1960s. Two groups of users burgeoned during that tumultuous decade. One was composed of rebellious high school and college students who bought into the "Make Love, Not War" idealism of the anti-Vietnam War movement. Some called themselves Flower Children. The others were soldiers who served in Vietnam, where marijuana was easy to get and commonly used both to counteract the boredom between patrols and to ease the strain of battle.

Smoking pot was so common among American troops in Vietnam that the army "began an all-out

BY THE 1960S, MARIJUANA WAS THE DRUG OF CHOICE AT LOVE-INS LIKE THIS ONE IN DETROIT'S BELLE ISLE PARK. FLOWER CHILDREN, ANTI-WAR ACTIVISTS, AND SOLDIERS IN VIETNAM ALL WENT TO POT. WHEN THE ARMY CRACKED DOWN ON MARIJUANA IN VIETNAM, MANY SOLDIERS SWITCHED TO MORE DEADLY DRUGS.

campaign to cut off the supply—with pot-sniffing dogs, searches of men's billets, and mass arrests for possession." Two years after the antipot drive began, the Pentagon sent investigators to determine how effective it had been. They found that it had been very effective indeed. Pot use among the troops had been greatly reduced. However, among the soldiers who had stopped using marijuana, "heroin—which was odorless, far less bulky than pot, and in Vietnam extremely inexpensive"— was now being widely injected. Heroin, which is extremely addictive, is a far more dangerous substance than marijuana.

Back in the States, however, marijuana remained the drug of choice. By the mid-1960s it was by far the country's most widely used illegal drug. It was estimated that there were a hundred pot smokers for every user of heroin. It was widely believed that grass (the generally used term for marijuana in the 1960s) was firing up the rebels on college campuses and that it played a major role in causing race riots in the country's inner cities. By 1968 the widespread use of marijuana had become a political issue. Two months before the presidential election, candidate Richard Nixon gave a speech launching the War on Drugs.

Woodstock

At first the War on Drugs wasn't taken very seriously by the grass users it targeted. They held smoke-ins at the Sheep Meadow in New York City's Central Park, on the University of California campus at Berkeley, in Lafayette Park in Washington DC, Lincoln Park in Chicago, and many other places. Pot was smoked openly at these events, and the smoke sometimes wafted over wider areas. Mostly, the police did not interfere or attempt to make arrests. But that would change with the creation by Congress of the Law Enforcement Assistance Administration, in 1968. The bill creating the agency provided money to local police departments. Although it was aimed at crime and street violence, drugs quickly became its main target. Marijuana became both the most obvious and the easiest drug to crack down on following the 1969 concert held in fields near Woodstock, New York.

Woodstock was a three-day rock and folk music concert and anti-Vietnam War protest. It was held on a dairy farm and attracted over 400,000 mostly young people. Tents were put up on fields that heavy rains quickly turned muddy. Conditions went from bad to worse with inadequate shelter, impure drinking water, and not enough food. All sorts of drugs were in evidence, and the wet air was thick with marijuana smoke. Through the clouds of smoke, cameras caught people streaking (the 1960s fad of running nude in public), making out, and indulging in many kinds of outlandish behavior. There was public outrage over the event, and it was strongly associated with the smoking of pot. The outrage fueled a crackdown on pot smokers and suppliers throughout the nation.

The Crackdown

Using, possessing, and selling marijuana had been a crime since 1937, but from the 1970s on, violations of the laws were to be prosecuted as never before. Marijuana was now regarded as a gateway drug leading to the use of more dangerous substances like crack cocaine and heroin. When the director of the National Institute of Mental Health said in 1971 that he thought marijuana offenders should receive light punishment, President Nixon was furious and suggested that he be fired.

A year earlier the National Organization for the Reform of Marijuana Laws (NORML) had been organized. Public opinion, however, was overwhelmingly against decriminalizing marijuana. This became crystal clear in 1973 when the New York State legislature passed a bill that provided harsh penalties for trafficking in drugs. The bill was dubbed the Rockefeller Drug Laws after New York's governor Nelson Rockefeller had fought hard to have the bill passed. A national poll showed that 66 percent of Americans—not just those in New York State—favored the laws. Among the penalties was a sentence of from one to fifteen years for possession with intent to sell one ounce of marijuana.

Creature Comforts

Do nonhuman animals use marijuana? According to psychopharmacologist Ronald K. Siegel, PhD, they do. Dr. Siegel, who has served as a consultant to the World Health Organization as well as to two presidential commissions on drugs, has spent many years studying the behavior of a variety of animals and their reaction to marijuana and other drugs. Among his examples are:

- lambs who graze in eastern European hemp fields seek out the riper marijuana plants to chomp on, and become "gay and crazy";

- captive pot-eating iguanas acting as alarm clocks for Mexican marijuana smokers who sit in a circle around the lizard until it collapses from overindulgence, the signal for them to stop smoking;

- flocks of sparrows that swoop down on newly ripened marijuana plants to gobble up all the seeds from the top branches and then fly away in a fluttering show of excitement and stimulation;

- a 1951 tragedy in which Greek army horses and mules gorged themselves in a pasture of particularly potent wild cannabis. They were so severely affected that eight horses and seven mules collapsed and died;

- rats and mice in police stations in San Jose, California, and San Antonio, Texas, that broke into sacks of confiscated marijuana and devoured the contents so voraciously that they were noticeably spaced-out.

Dr. Siegel has concluded that animals, like humans, instinctively seek out stress-reducing and pleasure-providing substances such as marijuana. Like humans, some animals regulate their consumption, and some do not. Like humans, some animals get high, and some suffer unexpected and disastrous consequences.

—*Source:* Intoxication: Life in Pursuit of Artificial Paradise
by Ronald K. Siegel, PhD

IN 1982, THEN FIRST LADY NANCY REAGAN ADDRESSED THE CONFERENCE OF THE
NATIONAL FEDERATION OF PARENTS FOR DRUG-FREE YOUTH. HER MESSAGE TO
YOUNG PEOPLE WAS THAT WHEN PEERS OFFERED THEM MARIJUANA, THEY SHOULD
"JUST SAY NO!" HOWEVER, IN THE YEARS IMMEDIATELY FOLLOWING THE SPEECH,
POT SMOKING BY ADOLESCENTS INCREASED.

In the early 1980s the Reagan administration decided that since marijuana was the drug most used by young people, it should be the main target of the War on Drugs. A campaign was launched to impress on the public that marijuana was a gateway drug leading to the use of harder drugs, such as cocaine and heroin. It blamed permissive parenting and hard rock music for encouraging marijuana use and its results. A University of Kentucky study showed marijuana to be "a cause of heroin use."

A best-selling nonfiction book called *Toughlove* advocated treating marijuana-smoking children as criminals. It spoke of breaking them of their "addiction" by sending them to jail. In keeping with its philosophy, treatment facilities sprang up in which young users were sometimes held forcibly. A more punitive facility, Straight, Inc., used techniques like denial of privacy, sleep deprivation, withholding food, and other forms of mental and physical abuse to stop kids from using marijuana and other drugs.

On July 4, 1984, the president's wife, Nancy Reagan, spoke at an elementary school in Oakland, California. She told the children that if peer pressure forced them to consider smoking marijuana, they must "Just say no!" This became the slogan of the Drug War over the next two decades, but it didn't slow the increase in marijuana use among young people. Throughout the 1990s pot smoking by eighth, tenth, and twelfth graders consistently went up, and is increasing still. As a slogan for the twenty-first century, Just say no! would seem to be just plain no answer.

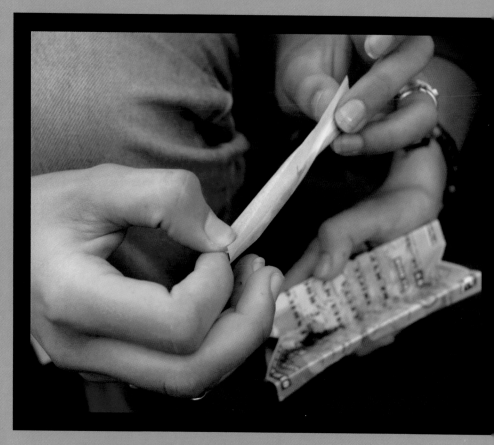

As the War on Drugs increasingly focuses on marijuana an opposition movement favoring legalization of the drug has been organizing. On September 1, 2001, in Berlin Germany, an annual Hemp Parade attracted thousands of supporters. Above, one of the parade's marchers demonstrates how to roll a joint.

2 Highs and Lows

A JOINT IS what users call a marijuana cigarette. What is the effect of smoking a joint? There is no one answer to that. Experts disagree. Studies disagree. Users disagree. Opinions and evidence collide, and anecdotal accounts contradict one another. The circumstances of use; the experience of the user, the source of the weed; the age of the user; the strength of the pot; the extent of use over both short and long periods of time; the health of the user; his or her psychological state; the bias of observers, commentators, experts, users; and other factors all may distort judgment and conclusions regarding the effects of marijuana. Nevertheless, judgments are made and conclusions are reached, and they should be considered and weighed one against the other in order to understand how marijuana does or does not affect people.

What it is, what it does

Marijuana is a green, brown, or gray mixture of dried, shredded leaves, stems, seeds, and flowers of the hemp plant. You may hear marijuana called by street names such as pot, herb, weed, grass, boom, Mary Jane, gangster, or chronic. There are more than two hundred slang terms for marijuana. Sinsemilla (*sin-seh-me-yah*—it's a Spanish word), hashish (*hash* for short), and hash oil are stronger forms of marijuana.

All forms of marijuana are mind-altering. In other words, they change how the brain works. They all contain THC (tetrahydrocannabinol), the main active chemical in marijuana. They also contain more than four hundred other chemicals. Marijuana's effects on the user depend on its potency, or strength, which is related to the amount of THC it contains. The THC content of marijuana has been increasing since the 1970s.

The way the drug affects each person depends on many factors, including:

- user's previous experience with the drug;
- how strong the marijuana is (how much THC it has);
- what the user expects to happen;
- where (the place) the drug is used;
- how it is taken; and
- whether the user is drinking alcohol or using other drugs.

Some people feel nothing at all when they smoke marijuana. Others may feel relaxed or high. Sometimes marijuana makes users feel thirsty and very hungry—an effect called the munchies. . . .

Some users can get bad effects from marijuana. They may suffer sudden feelings of anxiety and have paranoid thoughts. This is more likely to happen when a more potent variety of marijuana is used.

—*Source: National Institute on Drug Abuse of the U.S. Department of Health and Human Services*

Not a Pretty Picture

According to the National Institute on Drug Abuse (NIDA) of the U.S. Department of Health and Human Services, when someone smokes pot, "THC rapidly passes from the lungs into the bloodstream, which carries the chemical to organs throughout the body, including the brain." In the brain it connects to certain nerve cells and stimulates activity by them. This may affect thought, concentration, pleasure, time perception, and coordination.

Short-term effects, says NIDA, may include memory blocks, learning problems, distorted perception, unstable blood pressure, and increased heart rate. NIDA notes a study showing that the risk of heart attack quadruples in the first hour after smoking marijuana. (However, while NIDA's critics agree that marijuana use increases the heart rate, they point out that there is little or no evidence of heart attacks to confirm the extent of the danger.)

Long-term damage to the lungs from smoking grass is stressed by NIDA. They cite a 1993 study of more than four hundred frequent marijuana smokers who did not smoke tobacco and found that they had more health problems and missed more days of work than those who did not smoke pot. Many of the pot smokers' missed workdays were related to breathing problems. Even infrequent pot smoking, claims NIDA, "can cause burning and stinging of the mouth and throat, often accompanied by a heavy cough." Continual pot smoking can result in "a heightened risk of lung infections, and a greater tendency to obstructed airways."

A more serious result, according to NIDA, is that marijuana smoke may promote cancer of the respiratory tract and lungs. This is because marijuana smoke contains 50 to 70 percent more carcinogenic hydrocarbons (cancer-causing elements) than does smoke from tobacco. It is pointed out that pot smokers usually inhale more deeply and hold their breath longer than cigarette smokers and that this increases the lungs' exposure to cancer-causing smoke.

On the Other Hand . . .

Critics of NIDA begin with the fact that the institute is concerned with drug abuse rather than with marijuana itself. Because abuse is the focus, they say, studies are distorted and ignore those people who regulate their marijuana intake and suffer little or no ill effects. Many widely used and accepted substances focused on in terms of their effect on heart, lungs, and blood pressure might show similarly unfavorable results.

Salt raises blood pressure and may put a strain on the heart. Coffee, tea, cocoa, and some soft drinks contain caffeine, which may cause users to become nervous, irritable, apprehensive, restless, and unable to sleep, and to experience breathing problems and bone loss. Sugar, long believed to stimulate children and cause a high, doesn't really do that, but what it does do is contribute to obesity, pose a danger to diabetics, and it is also a major cause of cavities. Nutmeg and some other spices, according to Dr. Andrew Weil, a leading expert on alternative medicine, "contain compounds that affect the central nervous system."

Harmful, or Not: Pro and Con

A sampling of reports and opinions on the use of pot.

Lasting effect. Even after a day of not using marijuana, adverse cognitive effects—such as problems paying attention—can still be detected in heavy users of marijuana.

—Mayo Clinic Health Information

In strict medical terms marijuana is far safer than many foods we commonly consume. It is physically impossible to eat enough marijuana to induce death. Marijuana, in its natural form, is one of the safest therapeutically active substances known to man.

—Francis L. Young, administrative law judge of the U.S. Drug Enforcement Administration

Persons using this narcotic [marijuana] smoke the dried leaves of the plant, which has the effect of driving them completely insane. The addict loses all sense of moral responsibility. . . . While in this condition they become raving maniacs and are liable to kill or indulge in any form of violence to other persons, using the most savage methods of cruelty without, as said before, any sense of moral responsibility.

—1923, Emily Murphy, Canadian advocate of cannabis prohibition

By any of the major criteria of harm—mortality, morbidity, toxicity, addictiveness and relationship with crime—[cannabis] is less harmful than any of the other major illicit drugs, or than alcohol or tobacco.

—*March 2000 Report of the British Police Foundation*

Long-term marijuana use can lead to addiction for some people; that is, they use the drug compulsively even though it often interferes with family, school, work, and recreational activities; craving and withdrawal symptoms can make it hard for long-term marijuana smokers to stop using the drug.

—*National Institute on Drug Abuse*

Penalties against possession of a drug should not be more damaging to an individual than the use of the drug itself; and where they are, they should be changed. Nowhere is this more clear than in the laws against possession of marijuana in private for personal use.

—*1977, message to Congress from President Jimmy Carter*

Marijuana is taken by musicians. And I'm not speaking about good musicians, but the jazz type.

—*1948, Federal Bureau of Narcotics Commissioner Harry J. Anslinger*

Congress should definitely consider decriminalizing possession of marijuana.

—*Congressman and future vice president Dan Quayle*

Dr. Weil has studied drugs, including marijuana, and their effects for over forty years. In his book *The Natural Mind*, revised in 1998, he makes the point that marijuana "does not resemble any other known drug sufficiently to be classed with it." It is not, he states emphatically, a "mild hallucinogen" in the same general category as LSD, angel dust, or Ecstasy, which are hallucinogens. Marijuana is not a stimulant. At odds with NIDA's conclusions, Dr. Weil finds that while pot smoking causes a moderate increase in heart rate, reddening of the whites of the eyes, and dryness of the mouth and eyes, "no other clinically relevant effects have been documented, and it is unlikely that any will be."

Other medical authorities back up Dr. Weil's view. Recently a scientific advisory panel of the British government concluded that "the high use of cannabis is not associated with major health problems for the individual or society." The Canadian Medical Association agreed. *The Lancet*, an eminent scientific medical journal, proclaimed that "the smoking of cannabis, even long-term, is not harmful to health."

A Mood-Altering Drug

Just how harmful the health effects of marijuana use are remains an open question among U.S. doctors and other drug-abuse experts. That pot affects people's brains and alters their behavior, however, is not disputed, even by those who insist it is harmless. The National Academies Press, along with pot smokers and those who have observed them, reports that altered behavior includes a sense of well-being, increased talkativeness and laughter alternating with periods of introspective dreaminess followed by lethargy and sleepiness. NIDA chronicles a study of municipal workers that found those who used marijuana on or off the job were more likely to leave work without permission, space out and daydream at their desks, spend work time on personal matters, and goof off while performing tasks to which they were assigned. Other observable effects of being high on marijuana include dizziness, difficulty walking, fits of giggles or shyness, and an inability to remember things that have just occurred. According to "Marijuana: Adverse Effects," a paper issued by the Mayo Clinic, even twenty-four hours after using marijuana, heavy users may have trouble paying attention.

Studies of animals exposed to high doses of pot, particularly studies of monkeys conducted by Dr. Robert G. Heath, have led to the belief by some experts that marijuana kills brain cells. However, two later studies—one by Dr. William Slikker of the National Center for Toxological Research and the other by Charles Rebert and Gordon Pryor as reported in the *International Journal of Psychophysiology*—found no evidence of damage to the brains of monkeys exposed to marijuana for up to a year. Despite differences in the results of the studies regarding permanent brain damage, there is no doubt that marijuana is a mood-altering drug.

Mood-altering drugs are unpredictable. The

behavior that occurs from using them may depend on a variety of factors aside from the strength of the drug and the frequency of use, including even the genetic makeup of the person using the substance. NIDA reports that "scientists have found that whether an individual has positive or negative sensations after smoking marijuana can be influenced by heredity." In any case, mood-altering drugs, such as marijuana, often alter both perception and judgment.

Research and anecdotal evidence testify to a progression of undesirable consequences for young pot smokers in particular. Initial effects may include lack of attention in class, loss of interest in extracurricular activities, and generally spacing out. Continued smoking can cause a sort of vegetative state in which youngsters move away from healthy behaviors and distance themselves from family and even friends.

What follows is known as the culture of potheads. The user's grades begin falling off drastically. He or she withdraws into an isolation that is broken only by self-destructive contact with marijuana dealers and other potheads. Failure at school may lead to conflicts at home, and as the pressure increases, the young user begins to self-medicate to ease it. Marijuana is the drug of choice. It eases the pain of failure to function normally in many areas of the young user's life.

A Dangerous Combination

"Marijuana was a contributing factor in more than 110,000 emergency department (ED) visits in the United States" in the year 2001, according to the

Drug Abuse Warning Network (DAWN), a system for monitoring trends in drug-related emergency room visits and deaths. "Health Care Use by Frequent Marijuana Smokers Who Do Not Smoke Tobacco," a study conducted by the Kaiser Permanente Center for Health Research in Portland, Oregon, found that daily marijuana users had a 30 percent higher risk of injuries from accidents than nonusers. "Pot smokers should be aware that accidents are probably the number one hazard of marijuana," confirms no less biased a commentator than Dale Gieringer, coordinator of California NORML.

This "is scarcely surprising," Dr. Gieringer goes on to say, since marijuana can "degrade short-term memory, concentration, judgment and coordination at complex tasks including driving." Nevertheless, he goes on to point out that at least half the drivers involved in fatal automobile accidents have alcohol in their blood, as opposed to between 7 and 20 percent whose blood shows evidence of marijuana use. Complicating any conclusions that might be drawn from these statistics is the fact that 70 to 90 percent of those whose blood has traces of THC also have alcohol in their blood.

In cases involving both alcohol and marijuana, a National Highway Traffic Safety Administration (NHTSA) report concluded that alcohol was by far the more dominant drug-related cause of accidents. Another NHTSA study, "Marijuana and Actual Driving Performance," showed that the negative effects of marijuana on driving appear to be "relatively small" and less than those of alcohol. It noted that unlike alcohol, marijuana seems to make drivers more cautious. This may be because pot smokers are more aware of their condition and tend to compensate for it. The degree of compensation would, of course, have to do with the many factors governing the individual person. The lower the age of the driver, the less experienced he or she is behind the wheel, the more marijuana is likely to distort road judgment.

Are Potheads Addicts

Frequency of use and the amount of pot consumed may also be relevant to how accident-prone a marijuana user is. This raises some of the most controversial questions regarding the drug. Is marijuana addictive? Are frequent users potheads who are unable to control their habit? Are potheads not able to stop using pot? And, most debatable, what is an addiction anyway?

The World Health Organization (WHO) defines addictive drugs as those that "produce in the great majority of users an irresistible need for the drug, an increased tolerance to its effect, and a physical dependence as indicated by severe and painful symptoms when the drug is withdrawn." A distinction is made by WHO between addictive drugs and drugs that are merely habit-forming. The latter "cause an emotional or psychological, rather than a physical, dependence in the user and . . . can be withdrawn without causing physical harm or pain." In other words, physical dependency is addictive, while purely psychological dependency is simply a habit.

This is a tricky distinction. NIDA does not view it as a practical one. They point out that long-term marijuana use becomes compulsive, with no regard for how it may interfere with family, school, employment, and recreational activities. Putting a stop to pot smoking isn't easy. The craving remains, and there are withdrawal symptoms. Former pot smokers report that kicking the habit results in irritability, sleeplessness, and anxiety. Psychological tests reveal an increase in aggression during the withdrawal period. According to a 1999 study published in the journal *Psychopharmacology*, depression and appetite loss also occurred when marijuana use was halted. While most experts agree that marijuana is not physically addictive, a psychological dependency can and does occur in some cases.

Is Weed a Gateway Drug?

The second most disputed question about marijuana is its role as a gateway drug to more dangerous substances such as cocaine, Ecstasy, and heroin. A study published in the January 22, 2003, issue of the *Journal of the American Medical Association* reported that beginning marijuana use by age seventeen increased the likelihood of using other drugs and possibly becoming dependent on them. Long-term studies by George Koob, MD, of the Scripps Research

Institute led him to the conclusion that heavy use of marijuana causes the brain to release a chemical that increases under stress and could "lead to a subtle disruption of brain processes that are then 'primed' for further and easier disruption by other drugs of abuse," including harder drugs like crack and heroin. NIDA warns that "the risk of using cocaine is much greater for those who have tried marijuana than for those who have never tried it."

Disagreeing, a WHO investigation called the theory that marijuana leads to heroin use "the least likely of all hypotheses." An Institute of Medicine report stated that "there is no conclusive evidence that the drug effects of marijuana are causally linked to the subsequent abuse of other illicit drugs." Previously, in 2002, the British government had published research concluding that incidence of marijuana use progressing to abuse of hard drugs "is found to be very small."

Much of the evidence establishing a connection between pot and hard drugs comes from users themselves. Among those who view pot as a gateway drug, this evidence is most persuasive. Who better, they ask, to testify to the gateway effect of marijuana than those who have actually experienced it? In a January 2003 National Public Radio interview, nineteen-year-old former drug addict Nicole Scott related her experience, which gateway believers view as typical. "It was just kind of like because weed didn't get me high anymore,"

Nicole recalled, " so I went to the next drug, and it was coke. . . . I mean, like, my friend, she had it, so I tried it and then I, like—and then her friend was the dealer, so—then he started being my dealer and then I just started getting it from him all the time."

Was marijuana itself responsible for Nicole moving on to become a cocaine addict? Is Dr. Koob correct in his conclusion that it primes the brain for harder drugs? A study in the *Journal of the American Medical Association* suggests alternative explanations. One is that if initial experimentation with pot is pleasurable, as it often is, then it may simply lead to experimentation with other drugs promising to provide greater pleasure. Another is that although pot is illegal, the pot smoker has often suffered no legal consequences and is therefore likely to regard other drugs as equally punishment free. A third explanation—and possibly the most common experience—is that purchasing marijuana puts the user in contact with drug dealers, who also peddle hard drugs and promise even more enjoyable highs than weed can provide.

So, is marijuana a gateway drug? The answer is as equivocal as the evidence. The bottom line is that pot can be a gateway drug—but it doesn't have to be.

THE SUPREME COURT HAS RULED THAT MINORS IN SCHOOL HAVE NO PRIVACY RIGHTS AND THAT THEIR LOCKERS MAY BE SEARCHED BY LAW ENFORCEMENT OFFICERS WITH PERMISSION FROM SCHOOL ADMINISTRATORS. HERE A POLICE DOG IS BEING TRAINED TO SNIFF OUT MARIJUANA IN A SCHOOL IN HOUSTON, TEXAS. THE COMPANY TRAINING THE DOGS HAS CONTRACTS WITH FORTY TEXAS SCHOOLS TO SEARCH FOR MARIJUANA AND OTHER ILLEGAL SUBSTANCES.

3 Go Directly to Jail

MORE THAN 83 million Americans admit to having tried marijuana, according to the 2001 National Household Survey on Drug Abuse of the U.S. Department of Health and Human Services. In the year 2000, 734,497 people were arrested on drug abuse charges involving marijuana. Of these, 88 per-cent—646,042—were cases involving possession alone. They weren't sellers; they were users, part of the latest addition to the 83 million Americans who have sampled pot. They are the ones who make up the statistics that incite those who advocate legaliz-ing marijuana.

Mandatory Sentencing
One reason behind the increasingly large number of arrests for possession of marijuana is a law passed

by Congress in 1986 during the Reagan administration. That was the year that college basketball star Len Bias died of a cocaine overdose. House of Representatives Speaker Tip O'Neill, a Democrat, reacting to constituents' anger about Bias's death and to charges that Democrats were soft on drug-related crime, sponsored and pushed through the bill that would become the Anti-Drug Abuse Act of 1986. The act created mandatory sentences in drug cases—a five-year sentence without parole for possession of 100 kilograms of pot and a ten-year sentence without parole for possession of 1,000 kilos or more. For second offenses, the minimum sentences were respectively ten years and twenty years. For a third offense of possession of 1,000 kilos or more of marijuana, the sentence was life imprisonment.

Patterned after the stringent New York State Rockefeller Drug Laws, the federal law also became the model for legislation enacted by many states. In 1988 a second federal Anti-Drug Abuse Act was passed. It required employers doing business with any agencies of the federal government to meet certain requirements to maintain a "drug-free workplace." It also added a conspiracy rider to the original act. This rider applied the 1986 sentences to anyone who was a member of a "drug trafficking conspiracy." It made everyone in the "conspiracy" liable for every crime committed by it. In other words, a lookout for a pot pusher, or a so-called mule (someone who carries marijuana from one location to another), could receive the same punishment as the kingpin in charge of the drug cartel for which he or she worked. As members of the conspiracy, the small fry would receive equally punitive sentences.

After the passage of the conspiracy amendment, the prison population swelled. Within six years the number of drug cases in federal prisons increased by 300 percent. From 1986 to 1998 it went up by 450 percent. Acting assistant professor Inga Parsons of New York University School of Law, a criminal defense lawyer, puts it this way: "It's the person caught holding the bag, who usually is the poorest, who is given a hit to carry the bag. They are the ones most likely to be convicted."

The Weed and Seed Program

Enforcement of the Anti-Drug Abuse statutes within the borders of the United States has been the main thrust of the War on Drugs waged by federal and state law enforcement agencies for over thirty-five years. The war itself is worldwide in scope and deals with heroin, cocaine, crack, so-called designer drugs, as well as marijuana. In the United States, however, marijuana is the most frequent target for the simple reason that there are far more users of marijuana than of all the other drugs combined. Dan Baum, author of *Smoke and Mirrors: The War on Drugs and the Politics*

A SIGN NOTES DRUG-TESTING FOR JOB APPLICANTS AT A **H**OME **D**EPOT STORE IN **I**LLINOIS.

of Failure, points out that if marijuana were legalized, "there wouldn't be eleven million regular [monthly] users of illegal drugs in the United States, there would be two million."

Most of the eleven million are so-called recreational users, with only a small percentage among them using marijuana for medical reasons. The suppliers for these recreational users are the target of Operation Weed and Seed, a program started by the first President George Bush in 1992 as part of the War on Drugs. The program was designed to "weed" out neighborhood drug dealers and then "seed" the areas with antidrug education programs and social services.

The program was welcomed by many inner-city communities with serious addiction problems involving crack cocaine and heroin, but it also struck hard at middle-class marijuana users and sellers. Part of the money budgeted for Weed and Seed was allocated to state and municipal law enforcement agencies. Many of these agencies functioned in suburban communities, where the main drug used was marijuana.

One who was caught up in the Weed and Seed net was Jerry G., a nineteen-year-old student at Colgate University in Hamilton, New York. While pledging a school fraternity, Jerry G. was assigned to purchase a kilo of pot for a frat party from a dealer in a nearby city. The dealer turned out to be a narc, an undercover officer. Jerry G. was arrested and prosecuted under the New York State Rockefeller laws. "Because I had a whole kilo, they said I must be a pusher," Jerry G. remembers. "But it wasn't like that. It was just for the frat brothers. They chipped in for me to pick up the weed. I wasn't selling the stuff." He served all eight years of his prison sentence, can't afford to go back to college, and is having trouble finding a job.

Legalization: The Hot-Button Issue

Experiences like Jerry G.'s fuel concerns about whether marijuana should be legalized, as Dan Baum implied. There are some who would legalize not just marijuana but all drugs. Feelings run high on the issue. Jocelyn Elders, surgeon general of the United States under Bill Clinton, raised the question in December 1993. Speaking to the National Press Club on matters of public health, Ms. Elders remarked, "I do feel that we would markedly reduce our crime rate if drugs were legalized." She added, "I do feel that we need to do some studies."

Ms. Elders had already drawn criticism for advocating such controversial measures as a woman's right to choose an abortion, teaching birth control in the schools, providing condoms to young adult males and teaching them how to use them, and providing free needles to drug addicts. Now her statement favoring legalization of drugs drew a storm of criticism. Republican leader of the House of Representatives Newt Gingrich accused the

Clinton administration of being riddled with marijuana-smoking, "counterculture people." William Bennett, head of the DEA under the first President George Bush, demanded that Jocelyn Elders be fired. In the end, the criticism from members of both parties and others was so great that President Clinton dismissed her.

It was three and a half years later, on June 8, 1998, that a two-page ad in the *New York Times* raised the question of legalizing drugs. The letter was addressed to United Nations secretary general Kofi Annan and signed by more than 150 prominent Americans, including former secretary of state George Shultz, Harvard University professor and scientist-author Stephen Jay Gould, San Francisco mayor Willie Brown, Baltimore mayor Kurt Schmoke, TV and radio commentator Walter Cronkite, Episcopal bishop Paul Moore Jr., former New York City police commissioner Patrick Murphy, Hoover Institution economist Melvin Krauss, University of Pennsylvania law professor Lani Guinier, Harvard University professor Cornel West, executive director of the American Civil Liberties Union Ira Glasser, and many others. "We Believe the Global War on Drugs Is Now Causing More Harm Than Drug Abuse Itself" proclaimed the half-page headline of the letter-ad. The text went on to point out that "U.N. agencies estimate the annual revenue generated by the illegal drug industry at $400 billion . . . roughly 8 percent of total international trade."

It placed the blame for crime, violence, and corruption on "decades of failed and futile drug war policies." It called such policies "punitive prohibitions" in defiance of "common sense, science, public health and human rights."

Reform Options

The National Organization to Reform Marijuana Laws (NORML) has been the leading organization campaigning for the legalization of marijuana since its founding in 1970. They support legalizing it for recreational as well as medical use. They claim that pot is far less harmful than alcohol and tobacco, addictive substances that are sold legally. They point to the reduction in costs to law enforcement agencies, reduced contact between pot smokers and hard-drug pushers, and a reduction in violence among rival street gangs fighting over turf where pot is sold as some of the possible benefits that would be realized if marijuana were legal and could be purchased openly from merchants, as liquor and cigarettes are. They add that as with liquor, open sales by licensed providers would go a long way toward keeping pot out of the hands of minors.

Not just marijuana but all drugs should be legalized, according to the National Association of Criminal Defense Lawyers (NACDL). In a resolution passed in November 2000, the organization called for federal and state governments to declare "all drug use to be a health rather than a criminal

KEITH STROUP, EXECUTIVE DIRECTOR THE NATIONAL ORGANIZATION FOR THE REFORM OF MARIJUANA LAWS (NORML), SPEAKS AT A PRESS CONFERENCE IN NEW YORK IN APRIL 2002. STROUP FOUNDED NORML IN 1970. THE GROUP'S MISSION IS "TO MOVE PUBLIC OPINION SUFFICIENTLY TO ACHIEVE THE REPEAL OF MARIJUANA PROHIBITION SO THAT THE RESPONSIBLE USE OF CANNABIS BY ADULTS IS NO LONGER SUBJECT TO PENALTY."

problem and immediately repeal all laws criminalizing the possession, use and delivery of controlled substances." They recommended lifting all restrictions on the cultivation of marijuana plants. They advocated releasing all those held in state and federal prisons on drug offenses. Finally, they called for taxing and regulating the sale and use of all controlled substances.

Two-term Republican governor of New Mexico Gary Johnson also proposed safeguards for how legalization might work. He has suggested that marijuana be legalized first, that its sale be restricted to adults and strictly regulated, that the results be evaluated, and that only then should more dangerous drugs such as heroin and cocaine be made available. Safeguards for such hard drugs would include the requirement that they be administered with a doctor's prescription and in a hospital or clinic. "The more dangerous the perception of the drug," says Johnson, "the more control there would be." As for marijuana, "I don't want to see it in grocery stores," says Johnson. "Outlets would have to be monitored."

Obviously, there are differences in the way advocates consider legalization. Some, like Nobel Prize-winning economist Milton Friedman, propose "treating drugs as we now treat alcohol and tobacco: prohibiting sales of drugs to minors, outlawing the advertising of drugs, and similar measures." He believes that if the money now spent on the War on

Drugs "was devoted to treatment and rehabilitation . . . the reduction in drug usage and in the harm done to the users could be dramatic."

An approach known as decriminalization is favored by Arnold Trebach, director of the Drug Policy Center. Decriminalization is defined in a variety of ways by both advocates and opponents. It is also implemented in different ways by some U.S. states and some foreign governments that have passed decriminalization laws. In general, it means that there would be no criminal penalty for possession or use of small amounts of drugs. Technically, marijuana and other drugs would still be illegal under decriminalization. As Treback sees it, "all drugs could remain illegal," but there would be no prosecution for drug crimes not related to other crimes. Others envision decriminalization differently.

The Establishment Position

Opponents of decriminalization and legalization attack these options for a variety of reasons. The DEA claims that "misinformation is being presented by the sponsors of these expensive campaigns to legalize drugs." In its booklet "Speaking Out Against Drug Legalization," the DEA says that counter to the impression promoted by legalization advocates, the War on Drugs has been a success, as proven by the fact that drug use in the United States has gone down by more than one-third over the last twenty years. They insist that marijuana is illegal because it is harmful and contend that society would be ill-served if easily available pot were to be used by trainmen, bus drivers, emergency-room nurses, and others upon whom the public depends for its welfare. They stress the interrelationship between marijuana and hard drugs and between all drugs and crime and violence. As an example of the failure of legalization, the DEA cites Alaska. Possession of marijuana was legalized there in the 1970s, only to result in a doubling of marijuana use by 1990, when residents voted to re-criminalize possession.

Former DEA administrator Asa Hutchinson, taking issue with those who claim marijuana is basically a benign substance compared with tobacco and alcohol, pointed out that in 1999 a record 225,000 marijuana users sought help at substance abuse treatment centers. This was more than double the number seeking treatment seven years earlier. He also predicted that if pot were legalized, there would immediately develop a black market to provide it to underage users and others who could not get it under regulations or licensing practices governing its use. One of the chief dangers posed by pot, according to Hutchinson, is that "the level of THC, the addictive substance in marijuana, is much higher now than it was in the 1970s and therefore it's much more dangerous."

Increased THC levels were also cited by former drug czar William Bennett in a May 2002 interview with CNN. Bennett told CNN's Paula Zahn:

Well, this pot is coming from South America. It's coming from Mexico, and we're growing some here in the United States. This is very potent marijuana. As they say, this is not your father's marijuana or, for our generation, our friends in college's marijuana. It's ten to twenty times more powerful.

The heightened effect of modern-day pot and other illegal drugs were spelled out in a December 2001 speech by President Bush.

It breaks the bonds between parents and children. It turns productive citizens into addicts. It transforms schools into places of violence and chaos. It makes playgrounds into crime scenes. It supports gangs here at home. . . . Terrorists use drug profits to fund their cells to commit acts of murder. . . . And above all, we must reduce drug use for one great moral reason: Over time, drugs rob men, women, and children of their dignity and of their character. Illegal drugs are the enemies of ambition and hope, and when we fight against drugs, we fight for the souls of our fellow Americans.

Marijuana Arrests Compared to Total Drug Arrests in the U.S. (1980–2000)

YEAR	TOTAL DRUG ARRESTS	TOTAL MARIJUANA ARRESTS	MARIJUANA TRAFFICKING/ SALE ARRESTS	POSSESSION ARRESTS
2000	1,579,566	734,497	88,455	646,042
1999	1,532,200	704,812	84,271	620,541
1998	1,559,100	682,885	84,191	598,694
1995	1,476,100	588,964	85,614	503,350
1990	1,089,500	326,850	66,460	260,390
1980	580,900	401,982	63,318	338,664

—Source: Federal Bureau of Investigation, Uniform Crime Reports for the United States 2000, U.S. Government Printing Office, 2001

The Weed Killers

The U.S. Office of National Drug Control Policy (ONDCP) has officially designated areas within Tennessee, Kentucky, and West Virginia as the Appalachia High Intensity Drug Trafficking Area (HIDTA). ONDCP identifies this tristate area as "rural and rugged terrain with soil, temperature, and other climate conditions ideally suited for marijuana production." The area includes sixty-five counties within the three states, and it is "within easy reach of several large major population areas of the United States."

ONDCP has established an HIDTA program that coordinates efforts among local, state, and federal law enforcement agencies to put a stop to the illegal growing of marijuana in the region. The federal government provides equipment, technology, and other resources to further this goal. Manpower strength includes over a hundred full-time and nearly six hundred part-time personnel utilized during "intense concentrated enforcement periods."

The effort is to locate illegal marijuana farms in the region and destroy their crops. Pot growers are arrested and prosecuted. Actions are based on an ongoing system of collecting, sharing, and utilizing intelligence data relating to seed sales, cultivation products, specialized marijuana production tools, and other items.

However, the scope of the problem of pot production in Appalachia is extremely large. Marijuana

IN A DRIVE TO END THE PRODUCTION OF MARIJUANA, SONOMA COUNTY CALIFORNIA IMPLEMENTED THE CAMPAIGN AGAINST MARIJUANA PLANTING (CAMP). ABOVE, SPECIAL AGENT STEVE GOSSETT SEARCHES FOR MARIJUANA FIELDS FROM A HELICOPTER. CAMP AGENTS WIPED OUT OVER 7,000 PLANTS IN THREE GARDENS DURING A ONE-DAY RAID.

is the number one cash crop for the three states involved. In 1999 Tennessee alone wiped out marijuana plants valued at $628,226,000. This was more than the value of any other crop produced in the state. (Tobacco, which is legal, ran second, with sales grossing $217,429,000.) No figures are available for the value of marijuana crops not yet eradicated by the HIDTA program. Local people speculate that the illegal weed is still widely grown in the area, and will go on being farmed just as long as it is profitable.

SOME TWO HUNDRED EVENTS ACROSS THE COUNTRY, COLLECTIVELY KNOWN AS THE "MILLION MARIJUANA MARCH," WERE HELD ON MAY 4, 2000 TO DEMONSTRATE FOR THE LEGALIZATION OF MARIJUANA. ABOVE, A NEW YORK GROUP CAMPAIGNS SPECIFICALLY FOR ALLOWING POT TO BE USED TO ALLEVIATE VARIOUS ILLNESSES. PRO-MARIJUANA NEW YORKERS HAD BEEN ENCOURAGED BY NEW YORK MAYOR BLOOMBERG'S STATEMENT THAT HE HAD SMOKED MARIJUANA AND "LIKED IT."

4 Pot, Pain, and Punishment

A WIDOWED SIXTY-ONE-YEAR-OLD grandmother in New York City recently avoided arrest when undercover police collared a drug pusher in Washington Square Park. She had just finished buying a pack of twelve joints of Caribbean-grown marijuana. With the reefers in plain sight in her white-gloved hand, she was obviously guilty of possession of an illegal substance and subject to arrest and prosecution under the Rockefeller Drug Laws. "Why?" the detective asked her.

"I have abdominal cancer," she told him. "I go for chemotherapy twice a week. It makes me terribly nauseous and faint. My brain whirls. This is the only thing that makes it stop and makes the nausea tolerable."

The narc let her go.

Proposition 215

In California the cancer patient would not have had to rely on understanding and sympathy to avoid being arrested by state or local police. In 1996 a California voters' initiative approved Proposition 215, permitting marijuana for medicinal use. On the other hand, she could have been prosecuted by federal agents acting on the Bush administration's insistence that national antimarijuana laws overrule state statutes like Proposition 215.

Her quandary is typical of a group of people suffering from a variety of illnesses whose symptoms, advocates of legalizing medical marijuana insist, can be relieved by smoking pot. Opposing them are the federal government and various antidrug groups, who maintain that campaigns for legalizing medical marijuana are actually the opening gun in a campaign to completely legalize pot, and eventually harder drugs. While these are basic positions, the dispute over medical marijuana involves a number of unresolved subissues.

Among these are the role of marijuana as a treatment not only of cancer patients but also people with AIDS, glaucoma, multiple sclerosis, epilepsy, and those who experience chronic pain related to a variety of illnesses and injuries. There is also disagreement over whether marijuana is a useful tool in reducing alcohol and opiate addiction. Most recently, there has been a debate regarding marijuana's use in dealing with psychological disorders such as severe depression and devastating mood swings.

Benefits and Drawbacks

Two groups, cancer and AIDS patients, are in the forefront of the medical marijuana debate. Like the grandmother in New York City, many cancer patients treated with chemotherapy experience side effects of nausea and dizziness. Drugs that must be taken regularly by those with AIDS also make them nauseous, as well as causing stomach cramps and joint pains. Both groups experience extensive periods of appetite loss. Those who advocate legalization claim that smoking marijuana relieves these conditions.

A 1997 National Academy of Sciences (NAS) Institute of Medicine report found that marijuana has "potential therapeutic value" in cases of cancer and AIDS. However, it reported that "it also delivers harmful substances, including those found in tobacco smoke." In other words, while smoking pot might alleviate the agonies of cancer and AIDS treatments, it carried with it the risk of lung cancer and other unsafe effects. But these would be long-term effects, and cancer and AIDS patients are realistically more concerned with relieving their short-term pain.

The Psychology of Treatment

What are the psychological effects on patients of treating them with medical marijuana? According to "Marijuana and Medicine: Assessing the Science Base," a report released by the Institute of Medicine (IOM) of the National Academy of Sciences, they are mixed. No firm conclusions can be reached on either the psychological value or possible psychological harm of treatment with marijuana.

Patients who had never used pot experienced unpleasant feelings and disorientation after taking THC. These feelings were more pronounced in patients treated with THC orally—pills or liquid—than with those who smoked it. Previous pot smokers, on the other hand, were more likely to benefit, possibly because of anticipation that the marijuana would relieve anxiety, depression, or even physical distress. For those AIDS patients who had smoked pot before, marijuana often reduced anxiety, pain, and nausea while stimulating appetite.

The study granted that the effectiveness of marijuana in reducing anxiety, mildly sedating the patient, and producing euphoria could influence its therapeutic value. However, it also cautioned that these effects could be undesirable, and perhaps counterproductive, for some patients. It pointed out that the psychological effects of marijuana can complicate the interpretation of the drug's physical effects. Finally, it recommended that the psychological effects of the substances in marijuana be studied in clinical trials.

—Based on an Executive Summary of a 1999 report by the Institute of Medicine of the National Academy of Sciences

The DEA does not disagree that smoking marijuana may relieve pain in some cancer and AIDS cases. However, it cites a series of studies analyzed by the Mayo Clinic indicating that the same results can be obtained from dronabinol (also known as Marinol), a synthetic form of THC dissolved in sesame seed oil. Dronabinol, which can be prescribed as a capsule by a doctor, lacks many of the harmful ingredients of marijuana, and since it isn't smoked, it doesn't cause lung damage. However, the pill may be hard to get and expensive. Also it is slow-acting, whereas when pot is smoked, it provides quick relief.

The Investigational New Drug (IND) Program

Marijuana's status as an illegal drug was determined by the Controlled Substances Act of 1970. The act placed all illicit and prescription drugs into five so-called schedules. Marijuana was placed in Schedule I, defining it as having "a high potential for abuse, no currently accepted medical use in treatment in the United States, and a lack of accepted safety for use under medical supervision." Marijuana had been illegal to buy, sell, or use since 1937, but now it was specifically prevented from being prescribed by a doctor.

In 1972 the Bureau of Narcotics and Dangerous Drugs (now the DEA) was petitioned to reschedule marijuana so that doctors would be able to prescribe it. The bureau rejected the petition. The decision was appealed twice and last upheld by the U.S. Court of Appeals on February 18, 1994. Marijuana remains in Schedule I.

There was, however, an interesting exception— eight exceptions, actually—to the Schedule I ruling. In 1975 federal agents arrested glaucoma patient Robert Randall for growing marijuana. When the case came to trial, he defended himself on the grounds that marijuana was necessary to treat his condition. In glaucoma, intraocular pressure (IOP), within the eye, causes loss of vision and can even lead to total blindness. The THC in marijuana reduces IOP. Nobody knows how or why this occurs, but Randall was able to produce records from his own case that convinced the court to accept a "medical necessity defense" and to rule in his favor. As a result, the federal government established the Investigational New Drug (IND) program, enabling some patients to receive marijuana. The pot they received was supplied by the government.

Eight patients were supplied with marijuana from the IND program on a regular basis. However, in 1992, when word of the program spread and a flood of applications was received, the first Bush administration closed the program to new applicants. On December 1, 1999, the Clinton administration announced that the FDA would not resume taking IND applications for medical marijuana. However, the IND program still supplies the seven surviving patients it initially approved.

More States Legalize Medical Pot

A 1990 survey of oncologists (cancer specialists) reported that 54 percent favored making marijuana for medical use available legally, while 44 percent admitted to having broken the law by suggesting that a patient get it illegally. This was some of the background used in the 1990s by medical marijuana advocates who were carrying on their campaign state-by-state. Their first victories came in 1996 in California and Arizona, where voters decided in favor of ballot initiatives allowing pot to be used as a medicine and to be provided to patients in need of it. Medical marijuana legalization won in California by 56 percent of the votes cast, and in Arizona by 65 percent. Two years later, when the question was put on the ballot again, Arizonans confirmed the decision to legalize pot for medical use. Nevertheless, in 2003 Arizonans defeated Proposition 203, which would have decriminalized marijuana, not just for medical use, but entirely.

Since 1996, laws allowing marijuana for medical use have also been passed in Alaska, Colorado, Hawaii, Maine, Nevada, Oregon, and Washington state. On May 21, 2003, in Hartford, Connecticut, a medical marijuana bill was defeated in the state house of representatives by a vote of 79 to 64. One day later, Republican governor Robert Ehrlich of Maryland signed a bill into law that reduced the penalties for possession of marijuana when the marijuana was being used for medical purposes.

The Maryland bill had been opposed by the White House Office of National Drug Control Policy, which stands by the federal position that all state decriminalization or legalization of marijuana use for medical reasons is invalid because possession, use, and prescription of marijuana are illegal under Schedule I of federal law. In response, Robert Kampia, executive director of the Marijuana Policy Project, the largest pro-legalization of medical marijuana organization in the United States, praised Governor Ehrlich's courage in signing the bill. He went on to point out that recent polls showed that 80 percent of the American people approved of not imprisoning people who use marijuana for treatment purposes.

Federal Versus State Law

Conflict between federal and state authorities over the issue has been ongoing since 1996. Much of it has focused on California, where cannabis cooperatives were formed to grow and distribute medical marijuana. Under California's Proposition 215 many of the state's cities and counties enacted ordinances to permit the growing and distribution of marijuana for medical purposes. One of these was the city of Oakland, where street pushers and drug abuse were serious problems. Officials in Oakland decided that it would be better to offer pot to sick people in a regulated environment than to have them buy it illegally.

Politics as Usual

The battle over the legalization of marijuana for medical use from three different points of view:

Most Americans believe that medical marijuana should be available to help relieve the suffering of seriously ill patients, and eight states have passed laws to allow it. But the Bush administration has harassed medical marijuana patients in an effort to assert federal authority. This is another aspect of the drug war that should be ended.

—May 28, 2003, Ohio Democratic congressman and presidential candidate Dennis Kucinich

First of all, I don't call it medicinal marijuana, because there is no such thing. Marijuana is medical excuse marijuana. That's all it is. The pro-drug lobby is trying to use it to say it's a natural thing to do, to burn your lungs, ruin your mind. . . . It's just part of a marketing agenda.

—March 2001,Betty S. Sembler, founder of Drug-Free America Foundation

This is a huge conflict. State law legalizes medical marijuana and federal law makes marijuana illegal. Period.

—January 2003, Hallye Jordan, spokesperson for California attorney general Bill Lockyer

The federal government brought a lawsuit against an Oakland marijuana cooperative to stop the illegal distribution of marijuana. The suit, *United States v. Oakland Cannabis Buyers' Cooperative*, reached the United States Supreme Court in March 2001. The court decided that "medical necessity is not a defense to manufacturing and distributing marijuana." However, the ruling did not address the conflict between Proposition 215 and federal law. The question of whether the federal government could override a state law remained unanswered.

A little more than a year after the U.S. Supreme Court decision was handed down, the California Supreme Court ruled that medical users of marijuana enjoyed "limited immunity from prosecution under state law." In October 2002 the San Francisco Federal Appeals Court decided that the federal government could not revoke the licenses of physicians who prescribed marijuana. Issues of state versus federal jurisdiction were still muddled in January 2003 when Ed Rosenthal of Oakland went on trial in a San Francisco federal court on charges of growing marijuana and selling marijuana starter plants to other growers.

The Rosenthal Case

Ed Rosenthal was described by the *New York Times* as "the pothead's answer to Ann Landers, Judge Judy, Martha Stewart and the Burpee Garden Wizard all in one." He was a fifty-eight-year-old writer and publisher of self-help books that focused on marijuana. The charges against him arose because of a side business he ran—growing pot to be sold for medicinal use under the Oakland medical marijuana ordinance. He was, say his many supporters, "an officer of the city."

The DEA did not see it that way. Federal agents seized 3,163 marijuana plants from Rosenthal's facilities. They had also confiscated over seven hundred marijuana plants from the Harm Reduction Center in San Francisco, one of Rosenthal's customers. They regarded his operation as a thriving business and questioned whether its product would be restricted to strictly medical use. However, that was not the basis of the arrest. The basic DEA position was summed up by agent Richard Meyers, who pointed out that "marijuana is illegal regardless of the intended use, regardless of the person cultivating it, and regardless of where it originated."

Oakland city officials stood behind Rosenthal. Nathan A. Miley, a county supervisor who helped write the city's medical marijuana ordinance, pointed out that "Ed was just part of the whole effort" to make it workable. Rosenthal himself said that he had no idea that the city ordinance was "pushing the limits of the law." United States Attorney George L. Bevan Jr., who prosecuted the case, rejected that argument. He pointed out that "ignorance of the

THE SELF-PROCLAIMED "GURU OF GANJA (MARIJUANA)," ED ROSENTHAL WAS ARRESTED BY
FEDERAL AUTHORITIES FOR GROWING MARIJUANA FOR MEDICAL USE. ON JUNE 4, 2003 IN
SAN FRANCISCO, CALIFORNIA, AFTER HAVING FACED A POSSIBLE FORTY-YEAR JAIL SENTENCE,
ROSENTHAL WAS SENTENCED TO ONE DAY IN PRISON AND FINED $1,000. ABOVE, AFTER HIS
RELEASE, ROSENTHAL, HIS WIFE JANE, AND DAUGHTER JUSTINE ARE ALL SMILES AT A DECISION
REGARDED AS A VICTORY BY MARIJUANA ADVOCATES.

law or a mistake of law is generally no defense to a criminal prosecution."

Rosenthal was convicted and faced a possible forty-year jail sentence. A *New York Times* editorial pointed out that Rosenthal "was acting as an officer of the city," a fact the judge refused to allow the defense to mention at his trial. The editorial protested that "his harsh punishment shows that the misguided federal war on medical marijuana has now escalated out of control." It pronounced the "administration's war on medical marijuana" as "not only misguided, but mean-spirited."

There were other protests around the country. They had an effect. On June 4, 2003, U.S. District Court judge Charles Breyer sentenced Rosenthal. The sentence was one day in prison, allowing him to walk out of the court a free man because of credit for time already served and a fine of $1,000.

Where Do We Go From Here?

The sentence solved nothing. Rosenthal had been found guilty, but his crime had not been deemed serious enough to warrant a severe punishment. The question of just who should decide policy regarding medical marijuana, as well as how it should be decided, was still unanswered. Positions remained unchanged.

Regarding the right of California voters to decide to legalize medical marijuana, antidrug advocates continue to agree with Howard Simon, spokesperson for Partnership for a Drug-Free America. Simon has said that "voters should not circumvent recognized scientific and medical processes by deciding what constitutes safe and effective medicine via the ballot box. Let's not politicize it. . . . Let's let the scientists and researchers give us the answer— the same way the [FDA] would look at any other proposed medication."

Pro-legalization forces continue to believe that doctors, not the government, should decide what drugs to prescribe. They claim that the FDA policy regarding medical marijuana has been politicized and has little to do with the available medical evidence. The bottom line, advocates point out, is that existing cancer and AIDS patients suffering horribly when marijuana is unavailable.

Extremism in both camps clouds the arguments. Side issues proliferate. In the end, the issue of medical marijuana may not be resolved but only compromised.

ALARMED BY THE USE OF MARIJUANA AND OTHER ILLEGAL SUBSTANCES BY BOTH HIGH-SCHOOLERS AND YOUNGER CHILDREN, PARENTS HAVE ORGANIZED PATROLS TO KEEP SCHOOLYARDS AND SURROUNDING AREAS OFF-LIMITS FOR DRUG PUSHERS. IN MANY NEIGHBORHOODS THEY HAVE PRESSURED LOCAL AUTHORITIES TO PUT UP SIGNS LIKE THIS ONE WARNING THE PUSHERS AWAY.

5 Tests That Count!

ANYONE GOING TO middle school, high school, or college should be concerned with the second federal Anti-Drug Abuse Act, passed in 1988. The act was designed to apply to federal employees and to employees of firms that "contract with or receive grants from federal agencies." These firms were required to meet certain conditions for maintaining a "drug-free workplace." The statute ensured that goal by opening the door to testing for marijuana use.

Soon companies and organizations without federal contracts were also testing their employees for drug use. Their concern was that drug use, on or off the job, interfered with productivity. Early studies indicated that Monday job performance fell off among weekend pot smokers. Another concern was that safety might be affected. In factories, in particular, safety may depend on reflexes. The company, rather than the weekend pothead, would be liable for damages in such cases. After a spate of drug-related accidents, airlines, railroads, and bus companies began routinely testing pilots, engineers, and drivers for marijuana use.

In Loco Parentis

By the early 1990s concern about drug use was focused on young adults' use of marijuana. At the beginning of the decade, a spray kit called DrugAlert was being peddled to worried parents. The kit consisted of three aerosol sprays that turned color when they came into contact with surfaces touched by drugs. The idea was for parents to spray the desks, books, or personal possessions of teenagers to determine if they were using marijuana or other illegal drugs. When the American Broadcasting Company refused to run an ad for DrugAlert, director of programming Art Moore spoke for those concerned about the ethics of using the product when he said, "basically we felt it was an invasion of privacy."

This view conflicted with parents' rights and responsibilities to oversee the welfare of their children. These rights and responsibilities were—and are—automatically transferred to teachers and administrators in educational settings. They are

HIGH SCHOOL STUDENTS LINDSAY EARLS (*LEFT*) AND DANIEL JAMES, WITH THE HELP OF THE AMERICAN CIVIL LIBERTIES UNION (**ACLU**), SUED THEIR HIGH SCHOOL IN TECUMSEH, OKLAHOMA, OVER THE DISTRICT'S MANDATORY DRUG TESTING POLICY FOR STUDENTS PARTICIPATING IN EXTRA-CURRICULAR ACTIVITIES.

legally defined as *in loco parentis*, which translates as "the right to exercise parental authority in place of a parent." If a parent could search or test for drugs at home, then a teacher or school administrator could do so in school. That was the basis of the 1995 U.S. Supreme Court decision in *Vernonia School District v. Acton*. The decision upheld drug testing of student athletes because "students who voluntarily participate in school athletics have reason to expect intrusions upon normal rights and privileges, including privacy."

A few years later an Oklahoma school district went a step further. It required a urine drug test of all students in grades seven through twelve who signed up for extracurricular activities. A suit challenging the requirement was brought by the American Civil Liberties Union (ACLU). Student Lindsay Earls was a lead plaintiff in the case. "I'm really sad," she said, "that every other school kid in America might have to go through a humiliating urine test like I did just to join the choir or the debate team." In March 2001 a federal appeals court struck down the school's policy, calling it unconstitutional. In June 2002 the U.S. Supreme Court reversed the appeals court decision, in effect giving schools the right to test students.

Reasons for Testing

Is testing for marijuana and other drugs in schools justified? Whatever one may think regarding privacy issues and student rights, there is evidence to support such actions. Marijuana is by far the most used drug by people in their teens. According to a National Institute on Drug Abuse survey, the percentage of young people using pot increased alarmingly between 1992 and 2001. The survey found that nationally the percentage of eighth graders and tenth graders who had smoked pot almost doubled during that period and there was a more than 12 percent increase among twelfth graders. More than six times as many eighth graders and almost three times as many twelfth graders were using pot on a daily basis in 2001 as compared with 1992.

The survey found that 83 to 90 percent of the students in every twelfth-grade class polled from 1975 to 2001 testified that it was "fairly easy" or "very easy" to obtain pot. While the medical evidence concerning the effects of marijuana is controversial, the survey nevertheless determined that "students who smoke marijuana get lower grades and are less likely to graduate from high school" than their nonsmoking peers. Among students who scored the same on standardized tests in the fourth grade, twelfth grade test results were significantly lower for marijuana smokers. Among college students, attention, memory, and learning ability were impaired by heavy (defined as twenty-seven out of thirty days) use of marijuana. In drug treatment centers where marijuana has been the primary substance used by patients seeking help, 57 percent

Is Youth Going to Pot?

NINE-YEAR INCREASE IN 8TH GRADERS' MARIJUANA USE		
Frequency of Use	1992	2001
Ever Used	11.2%	20.49%
Used in Past Year	7.2%.	15.4%
Used in Past Month	3.7%	9.2%
Daily Use in Past Month	0.2%	1.3%

NINE-YEAR INCREASE IN 10TH GRADERS' MARIJUANA USE		
Frequency of Use	1992	2001
Ever Used	21.4%	40.19%
Used in Past Year	15.2%	32.7%
Used in Past Month	8.1%	19.8%
Daily Use in Past Month	0.8%	4.5%

NINE-YEAR INCREASE IN 12TH GRADERS' MARIJUANA USE		
Frequency of Use	1992	2001
Ever Used	32.6%	49.09%
Used in Past Year	21.9%	37.0%
Used in Past Month	11.9%	22.4%
Daily Use in Past Month	1.9%	5.8%

—Source: 2001 Monitoring the Future (MTF) Survey funded by the National Institute on Drug Abuse and conducted by the University of Michigan's Institute for Social Research had begun using it before age fourteen, and 92 percent before age eighteen.

A major concern is young adult pot smokers who drive. Under the immediate (and sometimes lingering) influence of marijuana, visual perception is distorted, motor coordination and reaction time are impaired, and the ability to think clearly is affected. It can be difficult to judge distances and to react to signals and road sounds. These effects may vary greatly from driver to driver, but they are greatest for inexperienced teen drivers. According to a National Highway Traffic Safety Administration (NHTSA) report, marijuana even in low doses negatively affects driving performance. The report adds that marijuana is the second most frequently found drug, after alcohol, in crash-involved drivers. NIDA has found that marijuana smokers show the same lack of coordination on drunk-driving tests as people who have had too much to drink. If school drug testing can reveal this before a student gets behind the wheel of a car, proponents of testing claim, lives may be saved.

This concern may be particularly valid when marijuana is mixed with alcohol or other drugs. One such combination can be found in a black market item called a blunt—a hollowed-out cigar in which marijuana has been laced with crack, cocaine, Ecstasy, or even embalming fluid. Since one can never be too sure just what a blunt contains, reactions can run from physical injury caused simply by lighting one up and taking the first puff to a hallucinatory trip during which there is a disconnect between thoughts and potentially harmful actions.

Blunts raise yet another concern for both parents and school authorities. Students who buy pot on the street are often urged by pushers to sample other varieties of weed, mixtures, and stronger drugs. This is the point at which the so-called gateway effect theory of marijuana may be valid. It is the point at which the adolescent pot smoker is most at risk from more addictive drugs. It is also the point at which he or she is being drawn—usually without realizing it—into a netherworld of crime and violence. The line has been crossed; face-offs with the law are on the other side.

The Process
There is strong evidence of a connection between the increase in drug use and the increase in violence over the last few decades. In the public mind marijuana is one of the drugs—perhaps even the most common—associated with violence. It is true that the distribution and sale of pot involves violence. Less well established is the connection between pot smoking itself and violence. In a general sense pot tranquilizes rather than incites. Those who would decriminalize it point out that the violence is a result of its being illegal, not of its use. Nevertheless, federal law links pot and violence through the Safe and Drug-Free Schools and

Communities (SDFSC) program, which authorizes the training of school security personnel to "interact with students in support of youth drug and violence prevention activities."

In-school drug detection is a major concern of the SDFSC program. This has been interpreted to include testing, as well as other tactics. A New Mexico school brought in drug-sniffing dogs to check out students as young as fifth graders. A school in South Dakota was said to have used dogs to scrutinize children in kindergarten. Other schools investigating marijuana use have tested urine, blood, hair, and/or saliva of students.

Urine testing is the standard NIDA approved method of determining if a student has used marijuana. The THC in grass is detectable in urine for two to three days after inhaling or swallowing pot. Habitual use can be detected in urine for up to twelve weeks, depending on the frequency,quantity, and duration of use.

The Office of National Drug Control Policy (ONDCP) spells out the four-step process of collection, screening, confirmation, and review for drug testing of students. A trained collector administers the test and observes while the student urinates, to prevent any substitutions. In cases where embarrassment or other circumstances interfere with urination, the collector stays with the student until he or she is able to comply with the test. The specimen is put in a container that the student must initial to verify that it is his or hers. It is then screened for the presence of THC or other substances indicating drug use. If the screening test is positive, a second test is done to confirm the result. Once the positive tests are confirmed, they are reviewed by a doctor or nurse with expertise in substance abuse in order to rule out legitimate prescription drug use.

Does Punishment Work?

There is no nationwide agreement on what the fate of the pot-using student should be after the use of marijuana has been established. John P. Walters, director of ONDCP, says that the purpose of drug testing "is not to trap and punish students who use drugs. It is, in fact, counterproductive simply to punish them without trying to alter their behavior." Many people believe that such students should be put into drug treatment programs rather than be punished, but the reality is that while such programs exist, there are far from enough of them to fill the need. Punishment, rather than treatment, is usually administered to the offending student.

Punishment usually means expelling the pot user. He or she is separated from the school community on the theory that the threat of luring others into using pot will be removed. Since the law has singled out students participating in extracurricular activities for drug testing, they are the ones most at risk of being expelled. Protesting such expulsions, Teachers Against Prohibition (TAP) points out that more than 50 percent of America's approximately 14 million high school students participate in such after-school programs.

TAP maintains that school-based extracurricular activities are actually a deterrent to drug use. They keep young people busy during those hours when they're most likely to get involved with drugs. The organization speculates that drug testing may force pot smokers to switch to harder drugs that may be more difficult to detect during urine analysis. Suspending or expelling the marijuana user, they say, will in the end create groups of "drug-using dropouts."

Testing Programs—Do They Work?

The purpose of testing is to reduce use of marijuana and other drugs. There is disagreement on how well that purpose is accomplished. Principal Lisa Brady of Hunterdon Central High School in Flemington, New Jersey believes that drug testing works very well indeed. She cites her school as an example. During the 1996-97 school year a survey taken at Hunterdon revealed that 33 percent of the school's 2,500 students had smoked marijuana. "This was just unacceptable," remembered Principal Brady. In July 1997 a drug and alcohol testing program of student athletes was instituted. Principal Brady said, "We had one of the best random testing implementations in the country." By 1999 the number of tenth graders reporting little or no use of drugs or alcohol increased from 41.8 percent to 47.3 percent.

Drug Use by Students in Schools With vs. Without Drug Testing Programs

Grade Surveyed	Marijuana use in schools that tested students for drugs	Marijuana use in schools that did not drug-test students	Other illicit drug use in schools that tested students	Other illicit drug use in schools that didn't test students
8th grade	15 percent	16 percent	10 percent	10 percent
10th grade	33 percent	31 percent	16 percent	17 percent
12th grade	37 percent	36 percent	21 percent	19 percent
High School	33 percent	37 percent	20 percent	18 percent

(male athletes only)

—Source: Journal of School Health and the New York Times

Principal Brady insists that drug testing was responsible for the reduction in drug use. "Nothing else had changed," she said. Despite success in September 2000, the school suspended all random drug testing. The ACLU had filed a lawsuit on behalf of students who claimed their Fourth Amendment rights were being violated. With the suit still pending, Principal Brady saw evidence that drug use at Hunterdon had begun to rise. Before testing started, she recalled, many people resisted the idea. "Now," she said, "parents are demanding that we test their kids."

Those parents believe that the test results are valid. Others do not. The ACLU states that "drug testing is frequently inaccurate, and there is no proof that drug testing has a deterrent effect on drug use." Support for this view comes from a large-scale national study published in April 2003 in the *Journal of School Health* of the American School Health Association.

The study of 76,000 students nationwide is by far the largest study ever conducted on the results of school drug testing. Financed by grants from NIDA and the Robert Wood Johnson Foundation, it collected data from 722 middle and high schools and surveyed 30,000 eighth graders, 23,000 tenth graders, and 23,000 twelfth graders. The study which tracked student behavior for nearly four years, suggests that drug testing in schools does not deter student marijuana use any more than no testing at all. Dr. Lloyd D. Johnston of the University of

Michigan, one of the researchers involved in the study, stated that drug testing is "the kind of intervention that doesn't win the hearts and minds of children. I don't think it brings about any constructive changes in their attitudes about drugs or their belief in the dangers associated with them."

Statistics produced by the study confirmed this. While 36 percent of twelfth graders in schools that had not tested for drugs had used marijuana in the previous year, in schools using drug tests, 37 percent had used pot in the previous year. Nineteen percent of twelfth-graders in schools with no drug tests had used other illicit drugs, while in schools that tested, 21 percent of twelfth graders had. The evidence was little different for eighth graders and tenth graders. Among the statistics for marijuana use by eighth graders was the finding that in schools with drug testing, 15 percent of the students reported using marijuana in the previous year; for schools with no testing, 16 percent reported using marijuana. Ten percent of both groups of eighth graders had used other illicit drugs in the previous year.

But some drug-use experts contend that the urinalysis conducted by schools is so faulty, the supervision so lax, and the opportunities for cheating so plentiful that the study may only prove that the schools do a poor job of testing. Even so, Tom Hedrick, director of the Partnership for a Drug-Free America, says, "at best testing could be a Band-Aid, and certainly not an answer."

Peer Pressure

What remains is the question of why young people use marijuana. There are no easy answers to this. The reasons may vary from person to person. Still, there are certain constants that pop up in too many cases to be ignored. The leading one is peer pressure.

There is more than one element to peer pressure. There's the *Don't be chicken!* sneer. There's the *Gonna party!* enticement. There's the *You're such a baby!* put-down. There's the *Trust me!* guarantee. There's the *It'll make you feel great!* promise. There's the *Everybody's doin' it!* invitation to be one of the gang. They all add up to wanting to be accepted by the group, regardless of where the group is leading.

Some young people are led into smoking marijuana by older siblings. Some see it on TV and in movies, hear songs about it, and conclude it must be cool to smoke a joint. It's part of the culture—their culture—and everybody wants to be part of their culture; everybody wants to be cool. Some smoke pot to escape family problems—quarreling parents, overbearing siblings. Some deal with rejection by a girlfriend or boyfriend by puffing a joint.

A few can't cope with life and smoke one joint after another to get away from it. Marijuana doesn't cause suicide, but teens with emotional problems are more likely to use pot and contemplate suicide. Drugs impair judgment. Coming down off a marijuana high can be depressing. Teen suicides are at an all-time high in this country. So is teen pot smoking. Pot doesn't cause suicide, but the connection is there to be made.

In the final analysis, marijuana is one of many substances that can harm the user. Some—candy, coffee, fast food—are less potentially harmful. Others—tobacco, alcohol, cocaine, heroin—are more potentially harmful. One joint won't kill the user. One joint too many may. It's not easy to judge the extent of the risk. In any case, there is a more important judgment to be made: consider how much there is to be lost.

Afterword

A prediction—

The relationship between young adults and marijuana will change over the next few years. It will change because the way America deals with pot is evolving. State after state is coming to accept the use of medical marijuana. Many local law enforcement agencies have opted not to devote scant resources to cracking down on pot smokers. Overcrowded prisons are pushing state governments toward reexamination of harsh sentences for marijuana-related offenses. Some legislatures are passing bills to reduce penalties related to grass. The idea that decriminalizing pot will decrease the street crime associated with its sale and distribution is gaining acceptance. Poll after poll indicates a swing in public opinion toward easing restrictions on marijuana use and enforcement of harsh drug laws. The signs point to some form of decriminalization or legalization on a limited basis.

Whatever the reform, there is agreement on all sides that marijuana should be kept out of the hands of minors. This may not sit well with young adults, but it is nevertheless valid. Minors simply lack the maturity and experience to intelligently use mood-altering substances such as pot. Just as there is a cutoff point below which one may not drink alcohol, drive a car, purchase cigarettes, or get married, so there must be one for using marijuana when and if it is legalized. Society has always limited the decision-making process for minors in a variety of ways. To smoke pot, whether it is legal or illegal, is a decision demanding maturity. If a minor smokes pot, he or she is breaking the law. That is just one more of the protections for minors designed by adults who care about them.

Glossary

addiction: A physical dependency on a drug.

cannabis: The hemp plant that produces marijuana and hashish.

DAWN: The Drug Abuse Warning Network, which monitors the health impact of drugs.

DEA: The U.S. Drug Enforcement Administration.

decriminalization: The removal of penalties for producing, selling, or possessing drugs, particularly marijuana, without actually legalizing such substances.

dronabinol: A capsule made from THC dissolved in sesame seed oil.

gateway drug: A "soft" drug, such as marijuana that leads to the use of a hard drug, such as heroin.

hashish: The most potent form of marijuana.

hemp: The plant from which marijuana is produced.

high: A euphoric reaction to pot or other drugs.

joint: The slang term for a marijuana cigarette.

legalization: Repealing laws banning sale and possession of all drugs or some specific drugs such as marijuana or medical marijuana.

marijuana: A substance containing THC, made from various parts of the hemp plant.

narc: Slang term for an undercover narcotics law enforcement agent.

NIDA: National Institute on Drug Abuse of the U.S. Department of Health and Human Services.

NORML: National Organization for the Reform of Marijuana Laws, founded in 1970.

Partnership for a Drug-Free America:
Organization in the forefront of the War on Drugs, which opposes legalization of medical marijuana.

peer pressure: Coercion by fellow minors to join in unwise activities such as smoking pot.

pot: A slang term for marijuana.

recovery: The path taken to stop using marijuana and other drugs.

recreational drug: A substance used for pleasure rather than out of medical necessity; also a term for occasional use of an illegal substance, as on weekends only.

reefer: A marijuana cigarette.

THC (tetrahydrocannabinol): The active chemical in marijuana that is responsible for the intoxicating effect on the user.

user: One who regularly smokes pot or uses other drugs.

WHO: The World Health Organization.

Further Information

Organizations to Contact

These organizations will provide information and help on marijuana and marijuana-related problems.

Al-Anon/Alateen
1600 Corporate Landing Pkwy.
Virginia Beach, VA 23454-5617
Phone: 888-4AL-ANON
www.al-anon.alateen.org/
E-mail: WSO@al-anon.org

Center for Substance Abuse Prevention (CSAP)
SAMHSA's National Clearinghouse for Alcohol
  and Drug Information (NCADI)
Parklawn Building, Room 12-105
5600 Fishers L.
Rockville, MD 20857
Phone: 301-443-0365
Fax: 301-443-5547
www.samhsa.gov/centers/csap/csap.html
E-mail: info@samhsa.gov

Common Sense for Drug Policy
3220 N St. NW #141
Washington, DC 20007
Phone: 717-299-0600
Fax: 717-393-4953
www.csdp.org
E-mail: info@csdp.org

Drug Enforcement Administration (DEA)
Information Services Section (CPI)
2401 Jefferson Davis Hwy.
Arlington, VA 22301
www.usdoj.gov/dea

Hazelden Foundation
PO Box 11, CO3
Center City, MN 55012-0011
Phone: 800-257-7810
www.hazelden.org
E-mail: info@hazelden.org

Marijuana Policy Project (MPP)
PO Box 77492
Washington, DC 20013
Phone: 202-262-5747
www.mpp.org
E-mail: mpp@mpp.org

National Council on Alcoholism and Drug
  Dependence (NCADD)
20 Exchange Pl., Se. 2902
New York, NY 10005
Phone: 800-269-7797
Fax: 212-269-7510
www.ncadd.org
E-mail: national@ncadd.org

National Institute on Drug Abuse (NIDA)
National Institutes of Health
6001 Executive Blvd., Rm. 5213
Bethesda, MD 20892-9561
Phone: 301-443-1124
www.nida.nih.gov
E-mail: information@lists.nida.nih.gov

National Organization for the Reform of
  Marijuana Laws (NORML)
1600 K St., NW
Washington, DC 20006-2832
Phone: 202-483-5500
Fax: 202-483-0057
www.norml.org
E-mail: norml@norml.org

Office of National Drug Control Policy
  (ONDCP)
Drug Policy Information Clearinghouse
PO Box 6000
Rockville, MD 20849-6000
Phone: 800-666-3332
Fax: 301-519-5212
www.whitehousedrugpolicy.gov
E-mail: ondcp@ncjrs.org

Advocates for Recovery
PO Box 460176
Denver, CO 80246
Phone: 303-639-9320
Fax: 303-639-9241
www.advocatesforrecovery.org
E-mail: afr@signalbhn.org

Charlotte Drug Education Center
1117 East Morehead St.
Charlotte, NC 28204
Phone: 704-375-3784

Partnership for a Drug-Free America
405 Lexington Ave., Ste. 1601
New York, NY 10174
Phone: 212-922-1560
Fax: 212-922-1570
www.drugfreeamerica.org

St. Michael's House
1759 West Adams St.
Chicago, Illinois 60612
Phone: 312-850-1099
Or 630-571-8722
Or 888-875-2470
www.stmichaelshouse.org/programs.htm
E-mail: info@stmichaels.org

SMARTMoves
Boys & Girls Clubs of America
1230 W. Peachtree St., NW
Atlanta, GA 30309-3494
Phone: 404-815-5700

The Jude Thaddeus Program
Saint Jude Retreat House
PO Box 657
Hagaman, NY 12086
Phone: 888-424-2626
Or 518-842-2204
Fax: 518-842-5099
www.soberforever.net/
E-mail: guesthouse@soberforever.org

Bibliography

In researching the subject of marijuana, the following books were consulted:

Baum, Dan. *Smoke and Mirrors: The War on Drugs and the Politics of Failure.* Boston: Little, Brown and Company, 1996.

Bennett, William J. *The De-Valuing of America: The Fight for Our Culture and Our Children.* New York: Simon & Schuster, 1992.

Earleywine, Mitch. *Understanding Marijuana: A New Look at the Scientific Evidence.* New York: Oxford University Press, 2002.

Gerdes, Louise I, ed. *Marijuana: Contemporary Issues.* San Diego: Greenhaven Press, Inc., 2002.

Gottfried, Ted. *Should Drugs Be Legalized?* Brookfield, CT: Twenty-First Century Books, 2000.

Hornik-Beer, Edith Lynn. *For Teenagers Living with a Parent Who Abuses Alcohol/Drugs*, Lincoln, NE: iUniverse.com, Inc., 2001.

Preston, Brian. *Pot Planet: Adventures in Global Marijuana Culture.* New York: Grove Press, 2002.

Sabbag, Robert. *Loaded: A Misadventure on the Marijuana Trail.* Boston: Little Brown and Company, 2002.

Schlosser, Eric. *Reefer Madness: Sex, Drugs and Cheap Labor in the American Black Market.* Boston: Houghton Mifflin, 2003.

Sharp, Elaine B. *The Dilemma of Drug Policy in the United States.* New York: Harper Collins, 1994.

Siegel, Dr. Ronald K. *Intoxication: Life in Pursuit of Artificial Paradise.* New York: E. P. Dutton, 1989.

Weil, Dr. Andrew. *The Natural Mind,* rev. ed. Boston: Houghton Mifflin Company, 1998.

White, William L. *Slaying the Dragon: The History of Addiction Treatment and Recovery in America.* Bloomington, IL: Chestnut Health Systems, 1998.

York, Phyllis, David York, and Ted Wachtel. *Toughlove.* New York: Doubleday, 1982.

Index

Page numbers in boldface are illustrations and tables.

107